Such Is My Confidence

Such Is My Confidence

By

CAROLYN RHEA

THE FAMILY INSPIRATIONAL LIBRARY

PUBLISHERS *Grosset & Dunlap* NEW YORK

FOREWORD

My purpose in sharing these simple convictions is that of urging everyone to define more clearly his own beliefs.

Examine yourselves, whether ye be in the faith; prove your own selves. *II Corinthians 13:5*

lest by any means . . . your minds should be corrupted from the simplicity that is in Christ.

II Corinthians 11:3

*"Such is the confidence that we have
through Christ toward God."*

Dedicated to

MARGARET

who had convictions

Contents

Such Is My Confidence

FAITH

Such is my confidence

Faith is the "white cane" for blind existence.

Beyond this single instant of life I am totally blind.

The maze ahead is obscured in darkness; each step holds potential terror.

But Faith goes before me to feel out the way that I might with confidence continue my journey.

Faith cannot see, but it can feel and conveys the message of having sensed the security of a safe surface upon which to tread.

Thus, with faith in my hand I need neither grope nor fear the terrors of darkness; for faith leads step by step along the path to God.

Such is my assurance

For we walk by faith, not by sight. . . .
II Corinthians 5:7

Whereas ye know not what shall be on the morrow.
For what is your life? It is even a vapour, that
appeareth for a little time, and then vanisheth
away. *James 4:14*

For now we see through a glass, darkly. . . .
I Corinthians 13:12

For therein is the righteousness of God revealed from
faith to faith: as it is written, The just shall live
by faith. *Romans 1:17*

For the Lord shall be thy confidence, and shall keep
thy foot from being taken. *Proverbs 3:26*

Blessed are they that have not seen, and yet have
believed. *John 20:29*

HOPE

Such is my confidence

Hope is a vase in which I arrange the flowers of
    health,
        happiness,
            prosperity,
                contentment.

Gaily I pluck lovely blossoms of brilliant hue and
    place them to my liking, then pause to admire
    their beauty and fragrance.

In reality the flowers are not always blooming, but
    nevertheless the vase is there in anticipation of
    some lovely arrangement.

Such is my assurance

And thou shalt be secure, because there is hope.
Job 11:18

But I will hope continually, and will yet praise thee more and more. *Psalm 71:14*

The hope of the righteous shall be gladness.
Proverbs 10:28

It is good that a man should both hope and quietly wait for the salvation of the Lord.
Lamentations 3:26

Now the God of hope fill you with all joy and peace in believing, that ye may abound in hope. . . .
Romans 15:13

Therefore my heart is glad, and my glory rejoiceth: my flesh also shall rest in hope. *Psalm 16:9*

And now abideth . . . hope. . . .
I Corinthians 13:13

LOVE

Such is my confidence

Love is like snow falling softly to earth.

It comes from above, for God is the divine source.

Love is impartial, enhancing both the lovely and the unsightly with new beauty.

Love is gentle, seeking neither to grasp nor to possess. Nestled under its soft blanket, even tiny green buds grow safely toward maturity.

Love is unselfish. Like melting snow, love unassumingly gives itself away to nurture those it touches.

Such is my assurance

Beloved, let us love one another: for love is of
God. . . . *I John 4:7*

Charity [love] suffereth long, and is kind; charity
envieth not; charity vaunteth not itself, is not
puffed up, Doth not behave itself unseemly,
seeketh not her own, is not easily provoked,
thinketh no evil; Rejoiceth not in iniquity, but
rejoiceth in the truth; Beareth all things, believeth
all things, hopeth all things, endureth all things.
I Corinthians 13:4-7

By love serve one another. *Galatians 5:13*

There is no fear in love; but perfect love casteth out
fear. . . . *I John 4:18*

My little children, let us not live in word, neither in
tongue; but in deed and in truth. *I John 3:18*

JOY

Such is my confidence

Joy comes only as a dividend.

It cannot be purchased outright nor accumulated through hoarded savings.

As I give my life unreservedly into the hands of God, He in turn reinvests it upon earth, spending freely where there is need.

Thus life—my only wealth—earns continuous dividends of spiritual joy,

And there is the certain knowledge that the investment itself is secure.

Such is my assurance

He that findeth his life shall lose it: and he that loseth his life for my sake shall find it. *Matthew 10:39*

Enter thou into the joy of thy lord. *Matthew 25:21*

Your heart shall rejoice, and your joy no man taketh from you. *John 16:22*

These things have I spoken unto you, that my joy might remain in you, and that your joy might be full. *John 15:11*

I know whom I have believed, and am persuaded that he is able to keep that which I have committed unto him against that day. *II Timothy 1:12*

everlasting joy shall be unto them. *Isaiah 61:7*

SORROW

Such is my confidence

Like lightning, grief strikes my life.

Its piercing impact momentarily paralyzes my mind,
but soon the reality of loss shatters the numbness
with torrents of despair.

At last the downpour diminishes to a drizzle. The
thundercloud passes; the sky clears—and soon
a lovely world smiles understandingly.

Lightning is an essential part of God's plan for clearing
earth's atmosphere; likewise, sorrow burns away
the dross so that only lasting values remain.

It is not finality. God is in control, using it in His
wonderful way for good.

Such is my assurance

By sorrow of the heart the spirit is broken.
Proverbs 15:13

The Lord shall give thee rest from thy sorrow. . . .
Isaiah 14:3

Sorrow is better than laughter: for by the sadness of
the countenance the heart is made better.
Ecclesiastes 7:3

For behold this selfsame thing, that ye sorrowed after
a godly sort, what carefulness it wrought in you,
yea, what clearing of yourselves. . . .
II Corinthians 7:11

And we know that all things work together for good to
them that love God, to them who are the called
according to his purpose. *Romans 8:28*

COMFORT

Such is my confidence

When something I love is taken from me—whether merely a toy or something of far greater value—just as a child, I cannot understand, and I cry loudly in protest.

Then it is that my Father calls me to Him that He might wipe my tear-stained face.

Gently He lifts me, rocking me in His strong arms.

Quietly He soothes my sobs and softly assures me that together we can make the loss a gain.

His spirit calms my own, and I view my sorrow with the serenity of new perspective. My Father has promised to help!

Tired and spent, yet filled with peace,

I rest in the security of His love and understanding.

Such is comfort.

Such is my assurance

Blessed be God . . . Who comforteth us in all our tribulation. . . . *II Corinthians 1:3, 4*

My grace is sufficient for thee: for my strength is made perfect in weakness. *II Corinthians 12:9*

Comfort ye, comfort ye my people, saith your God. He shall feed his flock like a shepherd: he shall gather the lambs with his arm, and carry them in his bosom, and shall gently lead those that are with young. *Isaiah 40:1, 11*

The Lord thy God in the midst of thee is mighty . . . he will rest in his love, he will joy over thee with singing. I will gather them that are sorrowful. . . . *Zephaniah 3:17-18*

Casting all your care upon him; for he careth for you. *I Peter 5:7*

DISAPPOINTMENT

Such is my confidence

As a knot appears unexpectedly in a thread, so dis-
appointment blocks the smoothness of life.

If a few deft strokes can untangle the skein, life
continues evenly; but if it cannot be corrected,
then it must be quietly woven into the design.

Thus the finished piece can still be beautiful—though
not perfect as originally planned.

Such is my assurance

I have learned, in whatsoever state I am, therewith to be content. *Philippians 4:11*

Now no chastening for the present seemeth to be joyous, but grievous: nevertheless afterward it yieldeth the peaceable fruit of righteousness unto them which are exercised thereby. *Hebrews 12:11*

Forgetting those things which are behind, and reaching forth unto those things which are before, I press toward the mark for the prize of the high calling of God in Christ Jesus. *Philippians 3:13-14*

PATIENCE

Such is my confidence

Patience irons the wrinkles out of life.
A newly laundered day soon loses its freshness,
    and the smoothness is marred by the creases of
        disrupted plans,
           misunderstandings,
               seeming lack of time,
                   clash of selfish desires;
But the warmth of patience, gently applied, will help
    the wrinkles disappear.

Such is my assurance

Let us run with patience the race that is set before us,
looking unto Jesus the author and finisher of our
faith. . . . *Hebrews 12:1-2*

Be patient therefore, brethren, unto the coming of the
Lord. Behold, the husbandman waiteth for the
precious fruit of the earth, and hath long patience
for it, until he receive the early and latter rain.
Be ye also patient. *James 5:7-8*

In your patience possess ye your souls. *Luke 21:19*

Knowing this, that the trying of your faith worketh
patience. But let patience have her perfect work,
that ye may be perfect and entire, wanting nothing.
James 1:3-4

HAPPINESS

Such is my confidence

Happiness is like a Christmas ornament.

Glittering and bright, it gaily decorates the tree, casting for a moment the spell of warmth and cheer.

Upon its bright mirror even drab, everyday surroundings are reflected in beauty.

Soon the season passes, and the ornament is tucked away. If chipped or broken, it is set aside without lingering regret, for new ones will take its place.

More likely, though, the gay little ornament, is carefully and lovingly stored that it might be enjoyed another season.

Such is my assurance

Thou hast put gladness in my heart. . . . *Psalm 4:7*

In the day of prosperity be joyful. . . .
Ecclesiastes 7:14

A merry heart doeth good like a medicine. . . .
Proverbs 17:22

He that is of a merry heart hath a continual feast.
Proverbs 15:15

Heaviness in the heart of man maketh it stoop: but
a good word maketh it glad. *Proverbs 12:25*

For thou shalt eat the labour of thine hands: happy
shalt thou be, and it shall be well with thee.
Psalm 128:2

If ye know these things, happy are ye if ye do them.
John 13:17

COMPASSION

Such is my confidence

As a sponge absorbs moisture, so compassion absorbs the trouble of those it touches.

Christ interpreted in human life God's compassion for mankind, and I shall seek to follow His example.

Concern for my neighbor must exceed mere pity. I will absorb a part of his trouble myself.

Such is compassion.

Such is my assurance

Which now of these three, thinkest thou, was neighbour
   unto him that fell among the thieves? And he said,
   He that shewed mercy on him. Then said Jesus
   unto him, Go, and do thou likewise.

Luke 10:36-37

Thus speaketh the Lord of hosts, saying, Execute true
   judgment, and shew mercy and compassions
   every man to his brother. *Zechariah 7:9*

Finally, be ye all of one mind, having compassion one
   of another. . . . *I Peter 3:8*

Bear ye one another's burdens, and so fulfil the law of
   Christ. *Galatians 6:2*

GREATNESS

Such is my confidence

Only God's microscope discerns true greatness.

Its lens brings into sharp focus one's total life. The deeds accomplished are seen within the context of one's heart, and the purposes which prompted them are laid bare.

That life is magnified which seeks humbly to serve as God's communication upon earth, sharing with mankind the blessing of God's knowledge, wisdom, compassion, and love.

Thus a man's own identity is merged with the greatness of God—outside of which, isolated human achievement is dwarfed to insignificance.

Such is my assurance

When I consider thy heavens, the work of thy fingers,
the moon and the stars, which thou hast ordained;
What is man that thou art mindful of him?
Psalm 8:3-4

And seekest thou great things for thyself? seek them
not. . . . *Jeremiah 45:5*

But seek ye first the kingdom of God, and his righteousness; and all these things shall be added unto you.
Matthew 6:33

I am the vine, ye are the branches: He that abideth
in me, and I in him, the same bringeth forth
much fruit: for without me ye can do nothing.
John 15:5

Let a man so account of us, as of the ministers of
Christ, and stewards of the mysteries of God.
I Corinthians 4:1

But he that is greatest among you shall be your servant.
Matthew 23:11

SUFFERING

Such is my confidence

With the skill of a make-up artist, suffering etches lines
of pain upon my life till my countenance assumes
the character of dejection.

Weary of such a wretched role, I earnestly implore
God to intervene. Compassionately, He reaches
out to me,

Deepens the faint tint of trust into a rosy glow,

Gently straightens the twisted lines of pain into those
of serenity, and

Deftly prepares my life, now disciplined by suffering,
for a new role of understanding.

HUMILITY

Such is my assurance

Remembering mine affliction and my misery, the worm-
wood and the gall. My soul hath them still in re-
membrance, and is humbled in me. It is of the
Lord's mercies that we are not consumed, because
his compassions fail not. They are new every
morning. *Lamentations 3:19-20, 22-23*

But the God of all grace, who hath called us unto his
eternal glory by Christ Jesus, after that ye have
suffered a while, make you perfect, stablish,
strengthen, settle you. *I Peter 5:10*

Because thou shalt forget thy misery, and remember
it as waters that pass away. *Job 11:16*

That I may know him, and the power of his resurrection, and the fellowship of his sufferings. . . .
Philippians 3:10

Wherefore let them that suffer according to the will of
God commit the keeping of their souls to him
in well doing, as unto a faithful Creator.
I Peter 4:19

HUMILITY

Such is my confidence

Humility is the threaded needle that sews the seams of
    life together.

Certain talents or larger pieces of the garment of my
    life would remain apart, sufficient unto themselves.

But until they are joined by humility to the lesser
    pieces of the pattern, my life cannot become a
    useful garment.

Such is my assurance

Be clothed with humility. . . . *I Peter 5:5*

If a man think himself to be something, when he is nothing, he deceiveth himself. *Galatians 6:3*

Humble yourselves in the sight of the Lord, and he shall lift you up. *James 4:10*

I therefore . . . beseech you that ye walk worthy of the vocation wherewith ye are called, with all lowliness and meekness. . . . *Ephesians 4:1-2*

He hath shewed thee, O man, what is good; and what doth the Lord require of thee, but to do justly, and to love mercy, and to walk humbly with thy God? *Micah 6:8*

COURAGE

Such is my confidence

Courage is the apron I wear for daily tasks.
It is no clumsy armor plate to don at times of danger,
  but simply a readiness to work at any task, however difficult or distasteful, knowing that God will
  add His strength to my efforts.

Such is my assurance

Be of good courage, and he shall strengthen thine heart:
wait, I say, on the Lord. *Psalm 27:14*

Be not afraid of sudden fear, neither of the desolation
of the wicked when it cometh. For the Lord shall
be thy confidence, and shall keep thy foot from
being taken. *Proverbs 3:25-26*

The Lord is my light and my salvation; whom shall I
fear? the Lord is the strength of my life; of whom
shall I be afraid? *Psalm 27:1*

I can do all things through Christ which strengtheneth
me. *Philippians 4:13*

SIN

Such is my confidence

Sin is voluntary rebellion against God. For a moment of selfish pleasure my mind elects to violate the sanctity of my soul.

Only as the pleasure decays into unhappiness do I fully comprehend the folly of my choice.

But He who shaped my mortal being knows the weakness of this human clay.

The glowing warmth of God's forgiveness becomes a new glaze which covers the cracks and restores a useful vessel.

Such is my assurance

Like as a father pitieth his children, so the Lord pitieth
them that fear him. For he knoweth our frame;
he remembereth that we are dust.

Psalm 103:13-14

But your iniquities have separated between you and
your God, and your sins have hid his face from
you, that he will not hear. *Isaiah 59:2*

Have mercy upon me, O God, according to thy loving-
kindness: according unto the multitude of thy
tender mercies blot out my transgressions. Wash
me throughly from mine iniquity, and cleanse
me from my sin. *Psalm 51:1-2*

Create in me a clean heart, O God; and renew a right
spirit within me. Restore unto me the joy of thy
salvation; and uphold me with thy free spirit.

Psalm 51:10, 12

FORGIVENESS

Such is my confidence

Forgiveness is the fire in which I burn my neighbor's transgressions.

Because our lives are so close, I cannot help seeing and feeling wrongs seemingly directed against me.

In the ensuing combat, however, love proves to be stronger than injured pride, and I toss the hurt into the flames to be burned.

Only then can I bring my own transgressions to God and ask that He too burn them in the blaze of His great love.

Such is my assurance

Lord, how oft shall my brother sin against me, and I forgive him? till seven times? Jesus saith unto him, I say not unto thee, Until seven times: but, Until seventy times seven. *Matthew 18:21-22*

And be ye kind one to another, tenderhearted, forgiving one another, even as God for Christ's sake hath forgiven you. *Ephesians 4:32*

Forbearing one another, and forgiving one another, if any man have a quarrel against any: even as Christ forgave you, so also do ye. *Colossians 3:13*

And forgive us our debts, as we forgive our debtors.
Matthew 6:12

Forgive, and ye shall be forgiven. *Luke 6:37*

JUDGING

Such is my confidence

Piously, I reach for the measuring rod to judge my neighbor.

Peering down from my towering height, I conclude that he is indeed a weak little person, measuring quite small against my stern rod.

But when I pull the rod away, I discover something strange indeed: I measure no bigger than my neighbor. My own height strikes the same mark at which I had measured him.

Humbly, I put my rod away and determine thereafter to measure with the cord of love, for it has no marks upon it.

Such is my assurance

Rejoice not when thine enemy falleth, and let not thine
heart be glad when he stumbleth. *Proverbs 24:17*

Therefore thou art inexcusable, O man, whosoever thou
art that judgest: for wherein thou judgest another,
thou condemnest thyself; for thou that judgest
doest the same things. But we are sure that the
judgment of God is according to truth against them
which commit such things. *Romans 2:1-2*

Judge not, that ye be not judged. For with what judgment ye judge, ye shall be judged: and with what
measure ye mete, it shall be measured to you
again. And why beholdest thou the mote that is
in thy brother's eye, but considerest not the beam
that is in thine own eye? Thou hypocrite, first
cast out the beam out of thine own eye; and then
shalt thou see clearly to cast out the mote out of
thy brother's eye. *Matthew 7:1-3, 5*

He that is without sin among you, let him first cast a
stone at her. *John 8:7*

HONESTY

Such is my confidence

Honesty is the keystone of moral living. Against its sharply chiseled form other pieces fit snugly together.

If I compromise with truth in relationships with myself, my fellowman, and with God, the keystone is marred. Constant abuse cuts deeply into the arch, and there is danger of crumbling.

As I adhere to honest principles, however, the structure of my life holds firm.

Such is my assurance

Let us walk honestly, as in the day . . .

Romans 13:13

Provide things honest in the sight of all men.

Romans 12:17

Now I pray to God that ye do no evil . . . but that ye should do that which is honest. . . .

II Corinthians 13:7

That we may lead a quiet and peaceable life in all godliness and honesty. *I Timothy 2:2*

ANGER

Such is my confidence

Anger boils within me as steaming water in a kettle.

Scalding words thrown indiscriminately upon the innocent as well as the offender will scald and scar.

Through self-control, I must keep anger contained within the kettle so that its blistering steam does not injure.

Such is my assurance

Be not hasty in thy spirit to be angry: for anger resteth in the bosom of fools. *Ecclesiastes 7:9*

He that hath no rule over his own spirit is like a city that is broken down, and without walls.
Proverbs 25:28

A soft answer turneth away wrath: but grievous words stir up anger. The tongue of the wise useth knowledge aright: but the mouth of fools poureth out foolishness. *Proverbs 15:1-2*

Make no friendship with an angry man; and with a furious man thou shalt not go: Lest thou learn his ways, and get a snare to thy soul.
Proverbs 22:24-25

Set a watch, O Lord, before my mouth; keep the door of my lips. *Psalm 141:3*

REWARDS

Such is my confidence

Eager for immediate, tangible rewards, I turn life into a carnival.

Attracted by the bright array of prizes lining its booths, I skillfully play its games and proudly accept the gay awards and loud acclaim.

Removed from the bright excitement and thronging crowds, however, I reflect in solitude upon what I have won.

The little rewards had indeed brought pleasure in spotlighting my achievement, but far greater is a word of praise from Him who unerringly judges eternal values and rewards accordingly.

Such is my assurance

For they loved the praise of men more than the praise
of God. *John 12:43*

Do not sound a trumpet before thee, as the hypocrites
do in the synagogues and in the streets, that they
may have glory of men. Verily I say unto you,
They have their reward. *Matthew 6:2*

With good will doing service, as to the Lord, and not
to men: knowing that whatsoever good thing
any man doeth, the same shall he receive of the
Lord. . . . *Ephesians 6:7-8*

Therefore judge nothing before the time, until the Lord
come, who both will bring to light the hidden
things of darkness, and will make manifest the
counsels of the hearts: and then shall every man
have praise of God. *I Corinthians 4:5*

MISTAKES

Such is my confidence

As I busily cut out the pattern for my life, sometimes the scissors slip and mar the lines.

Surveying the damage, I see the choices I may make.

If I brood and worry yet never do anything constructive about it, I permit the mistake to ruin all possibilities.

Perhaps I might trim the marred edges with further careful cutting and continue with the same pattern.

If the slip of the scissors has caused major damage, however, it is best to throw away the original pattern and immediately begin cutting a new one with a design that may prove better than the first.

Such is my assurance

A man's heart deviseth his way. . . . *Proverbs 16:9*

There is a way which seemeth right unto a man, but the end thereof are the ways of death.

Proverbs 14:12

He that refuseth instruction despiseth his own soul: but he that heareth reproof getteth understanding.

Proverbs 15:32

The ear that heareth the reproof of life abideth among the wise. *Proverbs 15:31*

Correction is grievous unto him that forsaketh the way: and he that hateth reproof shall die.

Proverbs 15:10

WORDS

Such is my confidence

Words are pins, in the cushion of the tongue.

Because they are familiar and inexpensive, often I am careless in using them and fail to consider that they can prick and wound.

I must remember that they serve a useful purpose and constitute a blessing when used as they were intended—to pin together the thoughts of my life with those of others.

Such is my assurance

The words of a talebearer are as wounds, and they go
down into the innermost parts of the belly.
Proverbs 18:8

Hold fast the form of sound words, which thou hast
heard of me, in faith and love which is in Christ
Jesus. *II Timothy 1:13*

Be thou an example of the believers, in word, in conversation. . . . *I Timothy 4:12*

In all things shewing thyself a pattern of good works.
. . . Sound speech that cannot be condemned.
. . . *Titus 2:7, 8*

Pleasant words are as an honeycomb, sweet to the
soul, and health to the bones. *Proverbs 16:24*

Whoso keepeth his mouth and his tongue keepeth his
soul from troubles. *Proverbs 21:23*

KINDNESS

Such is my confidence

Like a gentle breeze, kindness blows upon the scenes
of life,

Cooling overwrought selfishness and leaving a refresh-
ing awareness of the greater joy in giving than in
receiving.

Such is my assurance

And be ye kind one to another. . . . *Ephesians 4:32*

Charity suffereth long, and is kind. *I Corinthians 13:4*

In her tongue is the law of kindness. *Proverbs 31:26*

Add to your faith virtue. . . . And to godliness brotherly kindness; and to brotherly kindness charity. *II Peter 1:5, 7*

Be kindly affectioned one to another with brotherly love. . . . *Romans 12:10*

FRIENDSHIP

Such is my confidence

Stumbled upon along one's path, perchance as an
    interesting yet still rough pebble,
True friendship is polished
    by mutual ministries:
        of the spirit—in fellowship
        of the hands—in service,
Till its luster reveals the pebble to be a priceless gem.

Such is my assurance

Ointment and perfume rejoice the heart: so doth the
sweetness of a man's friend by hearty counsel.
Proverbs 27:9

A friend loveth at all times. . . . *Proverbs 17:17*

A man that hath friends must shew himself friendly:
and there is a friend that sticketh closer than a
brother. *Proverbs 18:24*

Greater love hath no man than this, that a man lay
down his life for his friends. *John 15:13*

Henceforth I call you not servants; for the servant
knoweth not what his lord doeth: but I have called
you friends; for all things that I have heard of my
Father I have made known unto you. *John 15:15*

MISSIONS

Such is my confidence

I am a missionary. My appointment came when I heard Him say, "Go and tell others."

I feel a compulsion to share my joy in Christ with those who touch my life.

Although my field seems very small, it does not lessen the glory of my calling.

The Holy Spirit sharpens my vision, and beyond the fog which enshrouds my little world I glimpse unlimited horizons.

My prayers can channel the impact of God's power into every corner of the earth.

Through offerings invested in the lives of God's representatives, I can go into all the world preaching the gospel to the lost everywhere.

Always there is the open door of opportunity and the confidence that Christ will go with me.

Such is my assurance

Now thanks be unto God, which always causeth us to triumph in Christ, and maketh manifest the savour of his knowledge by us in every place. For we are unto God a sweet savour of Christ, in them that are saved, and in them that perish.
II Corinthians 2:14-15

Go home to thy friends, and tell them how great things the Lord hath done for thee, and hath had compassion on thee. *Mark 5:19*

But ye shall receive power, after that the Holy Ghost is come upon you: and ye shall be witnesses unto me both in Jerusalem, and in all Judæa, and in Samaria, and unto the uttermost part of the earth.
Acts 1:8

Ye also helping together by prayer for us. . . .
II Corinthians 1:11

Go ye therefore, and teach all nations, . . . and lo, I am with you always, even unto the end of the world. *Matthew 28:19, 20*

HOME

Such is my confidence

The family is the divine pattern of existence. Each
family grows from the same pattern, yet each can
be quite different.

The quality of material, the choice of color, imagi-
native design, care given details—even trim and
accessories—all have a part in the finished effect.

Thus, the home becomes either a duplicate of mass
production or a fresh and exciting creation.

Such is my assurance

Through wisdom is an house builded; and by understanding it is established: And by knowledge shall the chambers be filled with all precious and pleasant riches. *Proverbs 24:3-4*

Therefore, whosoever heareth these sayings of mine, and doeth them, I will liken him unto a wise man, which built his house upon a rock: and the rain descended, and the floods came, and winds blew, and beat upon that house; and it fell not: for it was founded upon a rock. *Matthew 7:24-25*

Who can find a virtuous woman? . . . The heart of her husband doth safely trust in her. . . .
Proverbs 31:10, 11

Thy wife shall be as a fruitful vine by the sides of thine house: thy children like olive plants round about thy table. Behold, that thus shall the man be blessed that feareth the Lord. *Psalm 128:3-4*

BIBLE

Such is my confidence

The Bible is my spiritual authority.

Through its inspired writer God conveys His personal message to me and to the entire world.

It is the standard by which I can accurately measure every area of my life—a guide to the right relationship with God, with myself, and with my fellow man. When I am in error, it is my reproof and correction.

It is a tangible communication from God. I must read for myself to understand His message and then, with wisdom, translate it into living.

Such is my assurance

All scripture is given by inspiration of God, and is profitable for doctrine, for reproof, for correction, for instruction in righteousness: That the man of God may be perfect, throughly furnished unto all good works. *II Timothy 3:16-17*

For the word of God is quick, and powerful, and sharper than any two-edged sword . . . and is a discerner of the thoughts and intents of the heart.
Hebrews 4:12

But he said, Yea rather, blessed are they that hear the word of God, and keep it. *Luke 11:28*

I have laid up thy word in my heart, that I might not sin against thee. *Psalm 119:11*

Thy word is a lamp to my feet and a light to my path.
Psalm 119:105

EDUCATION

Such is my confidence

Education is a graph whose horizontal axis is World and vertical axis, Spirit.

Not all points of reference can be designated; only God, the author of all knowledge, comprehends its entirety.

My present life is a point of intersection upon the graph and pictures my relationship with the physical and social world as well as my relationship with God. It also charts my progress from the point of origin.

I must make certain that my life not only sweeps across the horizontal axis of worldly knowledge but also climbs skyward in spiritual growth; otherwise, the graph must depict an educated mind and an illiterate soul.

Such is my assurance

That the soul be without knowledge, it is not good. . . .
Proverbs 19:2

God is greater than our heart, and knoweth all things.
I John 3:20

Now I know in part; but then shall I know even as also I am known. *I Corinthians 13:12*

Brethren, I count not myself to have apprehended: but this one thing I do . . . reaching forth unto those things which are before, I press toward the mark for the prize of the high calling of God in Christ Jesus. *Philippians 3:13-14*

Who is a wise man and endued with knowledge among you? let him shew out of a good conversation his works with meekness of wisdom. *James 3:13*

That the God of our Lord Jesus Christ, the Father of glory, may give unto you the spirit of wisdom and revelation in the knowledge of him: The eyes of your understanding being enlightened. . . .
Ephesians 1:17-18

WORSHIP

Such is my confidence

Worship punctuates the sentences of life.

When joy is full, the heart *exclaims* its praise to the Giver.

Burdened with care, the mind *questions* earth's fleeting value and seeks the eternal.

In quiet moments of awe, the soul comes to a *full pause* before the majesty of God.

Such is my assurance

We know what we worship. . . . God is a Spirit: and
they that worship him must worship him in spirit
and in truth. *John 4:22, 24*

I will praise thee, O Lord, with my whole heart. . . .
I will be glad and rejoice in thee: I will sing praise
to thy name, O thou most High. *Psalm 9:1, 2*

Why are thou cast down, O my soul? and why art thou
disquieted within me? hope thou in God: for I
shall yet praise him, who is the health of my
countenance, and my God. *Psalm 42:11*

O come, let us worship and bow down: let us kneel
before the Lord our maker. For he is our God;
and we are the people of his pasture, and the
sheep of his hand. *Psalm 95:6-7*

Worship the Lord in the beauty of holiness.

I Chronicles 16:29

SOCIETY

Such is my confidence

I am a social being. I find pleasure in walking as a member of society and not always alone.

God planned it thus simply by placing many of us upon earth. I am not asked to give up my identity; rather, by identifying myself with others, my self can grow through their talents and understanding.

I have the responsibility of sharing myself in turn. Therefore, I must in every contact make certain that God is not misinterpreted through my human frailties.

Such is my assurance

They helped every one his neighbour; and every one
said to his brother, Be of good courage. So the
carpenter encouraged the goldsmith, and he that
smootheth with the hammer him that smote the
anvil, saying, It is ready for the sodering: and he
fastened it with nails, that it should not be moved.
Isaiah 41:6-7

And the Lord God said, It is not good that the man
should be alone; I will make him an help meet for
him. *Genesis 2:18*

Let us not therefore judge one another any more: but
judge this rather, that no man put a stumbling
block or an occasion to fall in his brother's way.
Romans 14:13

But whoso hath this world's good, and seeth his
brother have need, and shutteth up his bowels of
compassion from him, how dwelleth the love of
God in him? *I John 3:17*

CHURCH

Such is my confidence

The Church is my spiritual family.

As I accept the name of Christian, I become a member of God's family on earth.

Christ, foreseeing the need, established the relationship —a rock from separate grains of sand.

Within the church home, there is mutual love for each other. When one is weak, another lifts his burden. When one rejoices, the joy is shared by all.

Imperfect beings cannot constitute a perfect whole, but the union is sanctioned of God as a part of His plan for accomplishing His purpose on earth.

Such is my assurance

Having predestinated us unto the adoption of children by Jesus Christ to himself, according to the good pleasure of his will. *Ephesians 1:5*

We who are strong ought to bear with the failings of the weak, and not to please ourselves. *Romans 15:1*

If one member suffers, all suffer together; if one member is honored, all rejoice together. Now you are the body of Christ and individually members of it.
I Corinthians 12:26-27

I will build my church, and the powers of death shall not prevail against it. *Matthew 16:18*

GOVERNMENT

Such is my confidence

Democracy is the most favorable climate in which to nurture God's gift, freedom of choice.

Within it my worth is equal to that of each individual whom God has created, and I share an equal responsibility for making life upon earth worthwhile.

Therefore, I must faithfully execute my responsibility to myself and to my fellow man by building constructively upon God's physical and spiritual laws as I comprehend them.

Such is my assurance

And the Lord God said, Behold, the man is become as
    one of us, to know good and evil. . . .
Genesis 3:22

As free, and not using your liberty for a cloke of
    maliciousness, but as the servants of God.
I Peter 2:16

So speak ye, and so do, as they that shall be judged by
    the law of liberty. *James 2:12*

I exhort therefore, that, first of all, supplications,
    prayers, intercessions, and giving of thanks, be
    made for all men; For kings, and for all that are
    in authority; that we may lead a quiet and peace-
    able life in all godliness and honesty. For this is
    good and acceptable in the sight of God our
    Saviour. *I Timothy 2:1-3*

And Jesus answering said unto them, Render to
    Cæsar the things that are Cæsar's, and to God the
    things that are God's. And they marvelled at him.
Mark 12:17

GOD

Such is my confidence

God is the source of existence. He made the universe and gave it perspective.

I cannot set up my own equations and force God to fit them; rather I must seek to discover His.

God is my Father. In love, He breathed into me a spirit like unto His own—one which seeks communion with His.

He who fashioned my human form is ultimate Judge of His handiwork and

Will call me unto Himself and evaluate what was wrought in my fleeting years.

Such is my assurance

In the beginning God created the heaven and the
earth. So God created man in his own image. . . .
Genesis 1:1, 27

Whither shall I go from thy spirit? or whither shall I
flee from thy presence? If I ascend up into heaven,
thou art there: if I make my bed in hell, behold,
thou art there. If I take the wings of the morning,
and dwell in the uttermost parts of the sea; Even
there shall thy hand lead me, and thy right hand
shall hold me. *Psalm 139:7-10*

And will be a Father unto you, and ye shall be my sons
and daughters, saith the Lord Almighty.
II Corinthians 6:18

So then every one of us shall give account of himself
to God. *Romans 14:12*

Even from everlasting to everlasting, thou art God.
Psalm 90:2

God is greater than our heart, and knoweth all things.
I John 3:20

JESUS

Such is my confidence

Jesus is the human translation of God.

In finite form He interpreted the infinite God, who elected to make Himself known to us personally as Father through His Son, Jesus Christ.

Christ's healing hand was God's touch; His wisdom, God's voice; His love, God's compassion.

His death was God's plan to save me; His resurrection, God's promise of everlasting life.

Christ's life upon earth painted the simple picture of a son's faith in His Father, complete obedience to His Father's will, and spiritual maturity through acquiring His Father's knowledge and wisely using it to the honor of His Father's name. Thus He taught what my own relationship with God should be.

Such is my assurance

[God] Hath in these last days spoken unto us by his Son, whom he hath appointed heir of all things, by whom also he made the worlds; Who being the brightness of his glory, and the express image of his person, and upholding all things by the word of his power. . . . *Hebrews 1:2-3*

For I [Jesus] have not spoken of myself; but the Father which sent me, he gave me a commandment, what I should say, and what I should speak.
John 12:49

God was in Christ, reconciling the world unto himself. . . . For he hath made him to be sin for us, who knew no sin; that we might be made the righteousness of God in him. *II Corinthians 5:19, 21*

Knowing that he which raised up the Lord Jesus shall raise up us also by Jesus, and shall present us with you. *II Corinthians 4:14*

For I have given you an example, that ye should do as I have done to you. *John 13:15*

[69]

HOLY
SPIRIT

Such is my confidence

The Holy Spirit is God's energy at work on earth.
It is everlasting, for the Holy Spirit is God Himself. His
   works are evidenced in many ways:
   As a surgeon
   He cuts sharply into my sinful soul and
   exposes my need for Christ.
   As counselor
   He walks with me, helping discern the worthwhile from the debris.
   His strength
   supplements my weakness when complexities
   of life engulf.
   He is a broad shoulder
   to lean upon when my world crumbles and
   those I love are far from me.
   He gives the impulse
   for unselfish service in God's name,
   And the courage
   to speak my spiritual convictions boldly.

Such is my assurance

But ye shall receive power, after that the Holy Ghost
    is come upon you. . . . *Acts 1:8*

And when he [the Holy Ghost] is come, he will re-
    prove the world of sin, and of righteousness, and of
    judgment. *John 16:8*

But the Comforter, which is the Holy Ghost, whom the
    Father will send in my name, he shall teach you
    all things, and bring all things to your remem-
    brance, whatsoever I have said unto you.
                                            John 14:26

Likewise the Spirit also helpeth our infirmities. . . .
                                            Romans 8:26

and they were all filled with the Holy Ghost, and they
    spake the word of God with boldness. *Acts 4:31*

SALVATION

Such is my confidence

Salvation is the adoption paper by which I become a child of God.

God is perfect, and my sinfulness would mar His perfection. God is just; law requires that sin be punished. But God is merciful and accepts a substitute: Christ's death for mine.

As I accept God's provisions and gratefully acknowledge Christ in His role of saving me from punishment for my sin, I enter the relationship of becoming a child of God.

Though I disappoint God in countless ways, nevertheless He is truly my Father now and claims me for His very own.

Such is my assurance

God sent forth his Son . . . to redeem them that were
under the law, that we might receive the adoption
of sons. Wherefore thou art no more a servant, but
a son; and if a son, then an heir of God through
Christ. *Galatians 4:4-5, 7*

For all have sinned, and come short of the glory of God.
Romans 3:23

For the law of the Spirit of life in Christ Jesus hath
made me free from the law of sin and death. For
what the law could not do, in that it was weak
through the flesh, God sending his own Son in the
likeness of sinful flesh, and for sin, condemned
sin in the flesh: That the righteousness of the law
might be fulfilled in us who walk not after the
flesh, but after the Spirit. *Romans 8:2-4*

God standeth sure, having this seal, The Lord knoweth
them that are his. *II Timothy 2:19*

MYSELF

Such is my confidence

I am made in the spiritual image of God, my Father.

Equipped with the power of choice and spirit capable of communing with its Creator, I arrived upon an earth which is governed by God-established physical and spiritual laws.

My existence here is intended not to be merely a personal pleasure but a means of honoring my Creator. Stretching before me, at a beckon from God, is eternity—intimate communion with God which can be marred by a poor accounting of existence now.

As a child of God, I can best honor my Father by seeking to follow the example of Christ, in whom He is well pleased. Selfishness must be subjugated; love must be nurtured; faith must deepen its roots; God's will must become primary.

Only as I earnestly attempt to interpret and execute the Creator's blueprint can my life become the structure which the Architect foresaw.

Such is my assurance

So God created man in his own image, in the image of
God created he him; male and female created he
them. *Genesis 1:27*

But seek ye first the kingdom of God, and his righteousness; and all these things shall be added unto you.
Matthew 6:33

For we are labourers together with God: ye are God's
husbandry, ye are God's building. According to
the grace of God which is given unto me, as a wise
masterbuilder, I have laid the foundation, and
another buildeth thereon. But let every man take
heed how he buildeth thereupon.
I Corinthians 3:9-10

Every man's work shall be made manifest: for the day
shall declare it, because it shall be revealed by
fire; and the fire shall try every man's work of
what sort it is. *I Corinthians 3:13*

He must increase, but I must decrease. *John 3:30*

DEATH

Such is my confidence

Death is the dividing line between the numerator of present life and the unknown denominator of eternity. Only through becoming a part of the division process can I discover for myself the ratio —that full relationship which God has perceived all along.

Death is not a terror to be feared but a kindly instrument wielded in the hands of God, by which He brings a mortal into the joy of His immortal presence.

Such is my assurance

For now we see through a glass, darkly; but then face
to face: now I know in part; but then shall I
know even as also I am known.

I Corinthians 13:12

Then shall the dust return to the earth as it was: and
the spirit shall return unto God who gave it.
Ecclesiastes 12:7

Knowing that he which raised up the Lord Jesus shall
raise up us also by Jesus, and shall present us
with you. *II Corinthians 4:14*

Beloved, now are we the sons of God, and it doth not
yet appear what we shall be: but we know that,
when he shall appear, we shall be like him; for
we shall see him as he is. *I John 3:2*

Precious in the sight of the Lord is the death of his
saints. *Psalm 116:15*

PRAYER

Such is my confidence

Prayer is the gate which swings open to God.

Smugly secure within my fenced-in garden of existence, I kneel to enjoy it alone.

But there at my gate is God, inviting me to step outside for a moment with Him.

Reluctant at first, I slowly push it open till at last I can walk through.

The open gate of prayer affords the freedom of stepping out into fellowship with God and of viewing life from His perspective.

Such is my assurance

Lord, teach us to pray. . . . *Luke 11:1*

I will pray with the spirit, and I will pray with the understanding also. . . . *I Corinthians 14:15*

If ye abide in me, and my words abide in you, ye shall ask what ye will, and it shall be done unto you. *John 15:7*

In every thing by prayer and supplication with thanksgiving let your requests be made known unto God. *Philippians 4:6*

And this is the confidence that we have in him, that, if we ask any thing according to his will, he heareth us: And if we know that he hear us, whatsoever we ask, we know that we have the petitions that we desired of him. *I John 5:14-15*

PEACE

Such is my confidence

Peace is quiet confidence in God.

It is neither arrogant self-confidence, nor verbal boasting of belief, but serene trust which meets each crisis of life.

God—with infinite power, yet immeasurable mercy—is in control of the universe; and I have placed my life in His care.

Why should I fear my destiny?

Such is my assurance

Thou wilt keep him in perfect peace, whose mind is
stayed on thee: because he trusteth in thee.
Isaiah 26:3

Peace I leave with you, my peace I give unto you: not
as the world giveth, give I unto you. Let not your
heart be troubled, neither let it be afraid.
John 14:27

And the peace of God, which passeth all understanding,
shall keep your hearts and minds through Christ
Jesus. *Philippians 4:7*

In God have I put my trust: I will not be afraid what
man can do unto me. For thou hast delivered my
soul from death: wilt not thou deliver my feet
from falling, that I may walk before God in the
light of the living? *Psalm 56:11, 13*

I know whom I have believed, and am persuaded that
he is able to keep that which I have committed
unto him against that day. *II Timothy 1:12*

Our sufficiency is of God.

(*II Corinthians 3:5*)

Such is my confidence.